THE WHITE HOUSE

A BOOK TO BEGIN ON

THE WHITE HOUSE

Mary Kay Phelan   Illustrated by Ed Emberley

Holt, Rinehart and Winston
New York   Chicago   San Francisco

At 1600 Pennsylvania Avenue in Washington, D.C., stands a shining white house. It is the most famous house in America. The president of the United States lives there.

This house is the oldest government building in Washington. Yet it looks like one of the newest. Everyone calls it the "White House."

The president does not own the White House. It belongs to the government of the United States.

When he and his family move in, they bring only their suitcases. The furniture is already there. Some of it was left many years ago by other presidents. Now it, too, belongs to the government.

If the president is at home, a flag always flies from the roof.

When he goes away, the flag is taken down.

By watching for the flag, you can tell whether or not the president is in the White House.

There is no front door key to the White House. No key is ever needed.

Night and day, the White House police watch every gate and door.

When you go to Washington, you can take a tour of the White House.

On the ground floor are many rooms. One is the large kitchen. Another is the China Room where you can see the dishes used by every president's family.

There is also a broadcasting and TV studio on the ground floor. From here the president makes his speeches to the nation. This room was the first kitchen in the White House.

On the main floor a White House guide shows you the state rooms.

First, you will see the East Room, the largest room in the White House. It is gold and white, and very beautiful.

The president has his big parties in the East Room.

Next, you will walk through the Red Room, the oval-shaped Blue Room, and the Green Room. The president and first lady use these rooms for small parties.

You will see the State Dining Room, too. Sometimes more than one hundred people have dinner here.

As you leave through the main hall, you can see a wide stairway leading upstairs. The two upper floors are private.

The president's study is on the second floor. Bedrooms for the family and guests fill the second and third floors.

This is the White House today. Many years ago it was very different.

In 1789, our country was very new. George Washington had just been elected the first president.

Congress needed a place to meet. So the lawmakers decided to set up a new city.

The only business of this new city would be the government of our country.

Both the Northern and Southern states wanted the new city within their borders. But President Washington wanted to be fair to everyone.

Virginia

North Carolina

South Carolina

Georgia

He took out a map and found the exact population center of the time. It was a spot along the Potomac River.

This would be the fair place to build the new city. It would not belong to any state, President Washington said. And it should be called the District of Columbia.

In the new city, Washington thought
there should be a house where the
president would live.

Congress had a contest to decide who
would build the President's Palace.

Nineteen architects sent plans for this
house. James Hoban, an Irishman who
had settled in South Carolina, won the
contest.

In October, 1792, the cornerstone for the President's Palace was laid.

First the workmen put up strong brick walls, four feet thick. Outside the brick, they put gray sandstone.

Then came delays and more delays.

Eight years passed before the house was ready. George Washington was no longer president. The new president, John Adams, and his wife, Abigail, were the first to live in the house.

Ever since that day, it has been the first family's home.

When the Adams family came to the President's Palace, it was still not finished.

The house was designed with many rooms, but only six were ready.

There were no front steps, just an old wooden platform where the steps should be.

PRESIDENTS
PALACE

A few weeks later, President Adams'
grandson, Johnny Smith, came to visit.

The boy had a real surprise. He found
Grandma Abigail hanging up her washing
in the East Room. It was still just four
brick walls.

Mrs. Adams was the only president's
wife who ever used the East Room for
drying clothes.

Our third president, Thomas Jefferson, came to live in the house in 1801. By now most of the rooms were finished.

Mr. Jefferson did not like the name, the President's Palace. He thought it sounded too much like the home of a king.

Instead, President Jefferson said the house should be called the President's House.

One day President Jefferson told his six grandchildren that he had an exciting surprise for them.

The surprise was a new baby brother.

James Madison Randolph was the first baby born in the President's House.

While the next president, James Madison, lived in the house, there were many gay parties.

Mrs. Madison gave the first egg-rolling party on the Monday after Easter. She dyed hundreds of eggs herself. Then she asked all the children in Washington to come to the Capitol grounds.

As the boys and girls rolled their eggs down the wide green lawns, Mrs. Madison may have decided that this was the best party she had ever given.

In 1812 the United States went to war with England.

On August 24, 1814, British soldiers marched into Washington. They set fire to the President's House. The fire burned all night.

The next day a great storm put out the fire. But only the outside walls were left standing.

Congress asked James Hoban to rebuild the President's House. Three years passed. By that time James Monroe was president.

The Monroe family moved into the house while it was still being painted. The fresh, white paint covered up the black marks left by the fire.

Soon everyone was calling it the White House.

President Monroe added something
new to the shining white house. It was a
wide porch on the south side. There were
broad, sweeping steps leading up to the
porch.

The new porch was called the South
Portico. It was finished in time for the
wedding of the President's daughter,
Maria.

John Quincy Adams followed President Monroe into the White House. During the summer of 1825, President Adams had a famous visitor, the Marquis de Lafayette, from France.

Lafayette had been on a tour of the United States. Someone had given him a live alligator.

While the famous Frenchman visited President Adams, the alligator lived in the East Room.

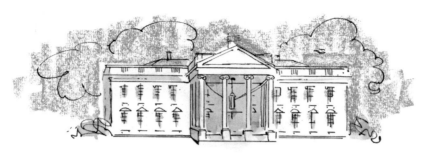

During the next few years several changes were made in the big white house.

After Andrew Jackson became president, the East Room was finished. He used it for his parties.

Then the President added a square porch on the north side. It was called the North Portico.

All important visitors should use the North Portico entrance, President Jackson decided.

This is still true, today.

In 1861, the sixteenth president, Abraham Lincoln, brought his family to the White House. A month later the Civil War began.

The kindly President had many problems. But he was never too busy to go to the attic and watch his sons, Willie and Tad, give a play.

Mr. Lincoln was glad to pay five cents for his ticket. It was worth it, he said, because he laughed so hard at the boys' jokes.

Tad's favorite pets were a pair of goats.

Sometimes he would hitch the goats to a kitchen chair. Then he would ride around and around the East Room.

Several years after the Civil War, a famous general, Ulysses S. Grant, became president.

Christmas, 1871, was a big day for his son, Jesse. Jesse's gang held its first meeting in the White House gardener's old toolhouse.

The name of the gang was the K.F.R. Society. The meaning of the letters was a deep, dark secret.

But President Grant always called it the "Kick, Fight, and Run Society."

Four years later, the White House was again filled with boys.

Irvin and Abram were two of President and Mrs. James Garfield's sons. When their parents were out, the boys had bike races in the East Room.

From the top of the stairs, Irvin used to warn everyone to get out of his way.

The next minute he would zoom down the wide stairs on his high-wheeled bike.

President and Mrs. Theodore Roosevelt came to the White House in 1901. With them came their six children: Alice, Theodore, Jr., Kermit, Ethel, Archie, and Quentin.

Something doing every minute was the rule in the shining white house for the next eight years. And all of it was fun!

All the younger children had stilts. No steps were too steep for a noisy race.

No furniture was too fine for a wild game of leapfrog.

Animals were everywhere, often on the best furniture. Many a visitor had to be careful not to sit on a pet snake.

And there was almost always a pillow fight with Father before bedtime.

One day Archie had the measles.
Quentin smuggled the pony, Algonquin,
into the White House elevator.

Up they rode to the second floor.

When Archie saw his pony, he felt
much better. In fact, he was sure that
seeing Algonquin would cure his measles!

By 1902 the White House was more than one hundred years old.

Outside, the walls were still strong and sturdy.

But inside, there were cracks in the ceiling. And the wallpaper was peeling off.

Congress decided to make some repairs. The Roosevelts moved out, and the workmen moved in.

Four months later, the house was again ready for the Roosevelts.

Inside, there were more bedrooms. The cracks had been fixed. There was new wallpaper in many rooms.

Outside, the walls had a fresh coat of white paint. President Roosevelt asked Congress to pass a special law about the name of the house.

Congress did. Since 1902, the official name of the President's House has been the White House.

President William Howard Taft and his family followed the Roosevelts into the White House.

The oldest son, Robert, was away at school most of the time. But the younger children, Charlie and Helen, had many good times there.

Sometimes they got big tin trays from the kitchen. Then they climbed to the top of the wide stairway. Sitting on the trays, they bumped all the way to the bottom.

During World War I, President Woodrow Wilson lived in the White House.

Many workmen had gone to war. Mrs. Wilson could find no one to cut the grass.

So she bought a number of sheep and put them out to graze on the White House lawn. These sheep kept the grass neat and trim.

After President Wilson left, Warren G. Harding came to the White House. Calvin Coolidge and Herbert Hoover followed.

Next was Franklin D. Roosevelt, who lived there for twelve years—longer than any other president.

He was there during World War II, when the house looked very different.

Blackout curtains were placed at the windows. Machine guns were mounted on the roof. Soldiers patrolled the walks around the house.

An air-raid shelter was built for the President and his family.

Harry S. Truman was the next president. After living in the White House awhile, he began to hear strange cracking noises.

Men came to look over the old house. They listened to the noises and decided the house was not safe.

Congress agreed to build a new house. But they would build it inside the old walls, which were still strong.

Slowly, carefully, the old house was taken apart.

Men took many, many photographs. They made drawings and more drawings.

The builders wanted to be sure of one thing. The state rooms must look exactly the same in the new house. Nothing could be different.

Then the bulldozers moved in.

A two-story basement was dug under the ground floor.

The old wooden beams were taken down. A new steel framework was put up.

Now the house would be strong and solid.

One by one, the state rooms were rebuilt. Each room looked very much as it had before.

Even the same doorknobs were used.

On the second and third floors, more bedrooms were added. A family sunroom was built above the South Portico.

Four years went by before the new White House was ready. It had cost almost six million dollars.

President Truman lived there only one year before Dwight D. Eisenhower and his wife, Mamie, came.

The Eisenhower grandchildren often visited at the White House. David liked to practice his golf shots on the south grounds with his grandfather.

The new White House has 132 rooms and 20 baths and showers.

It takes many people to keep such a big house running smoothly. Seventy people come to the White House every day to help with the work.

There are cooks and carpenters, housemen and butlers, electricians and maids, painters and gardeners.

By 1961, a new president, John F. Kennedy and his wife, Jacqueline, moved in. With them came Caroline, and her baby brother, John, Jr.

Many important people visit the White House each year. They come from all over the world.

In the spring of 1961, President Kennedy's daughter, Caroline, watched a helicopter land on the South Grounds.

Out stepped Commander Alan Shepard, America's first spaceman. He, too, had come to visit the White House.

Some people say that the new White House is so strong, it will be standing two hundred years from now.

If it is, it will continue to be the most famous home in all America.

It will still be the one house that belongs to each and every one of us.

ABOUT THE AUTHOR AND ARTIST

MARY KAY PHELAN lives in Davenport, Iowa. *The White House* is her first book. It grew out of a trip to Washington, D.C., with her two sons. Four visits to the capital in the past few years have convinced her there is enough history in Washington to keep her writing for the rest of her life. She was graduated from DePauw University and holds an M.A. from Northwestern University. She now works with her husband, editing the historical films his company produces.

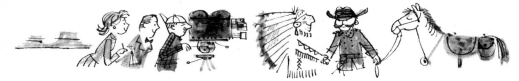

ED EMBERLEY was graduated from the Massachusetts School of Art. He has written and illustrated one children's book, and is at work on several more. He likes to make wood engravings and print limited editions of books on his small hand press. With his wife and young children, he lives on the north shore of Massachusetts. Someday he hopes to have a sailboat, an antique car, a big sheep dog, and an old house with a huge barn where he can write and illustrate books.